BLOOD OF STONE

T0170644

Copyright © 2024 Tāriq Malik

01 02 03 04 05 28 27 26 25 24

All rights reserved. No part of this publication may be reproduced, stored in a retrieval system or transmitted, in any form or by any means, without prior permission of the publisher or, in the case of photocopying or other reprographic copying, a licence from Access Copyright, the Canadian Copyright Licensing Agency, www.accesscopyright.ca, 1-800-893-5777, info@accesscopyright.ca.

Caitlin Press Inc.

3375 Ponderosa Way

Qualicum Beach, BC V9K 2J8

www.caitlinpress.com

Text and cover design by Vici Johnstone

Printed in Canada

All images from the author's personal family collection.

Image on cover and page 66 by Mohammed Sadiq Mughal, courtesy Ashfaq Mughal

Caitlin Press Inc. acknowledges financial support from the Government of Canada and the Canada Council for the Arts, and the Province of British Columbia through the British Columbia Arts Council and the Book Publisher's Tax Credit.

Library and Archives Canada Cataloguing in Publication

Title: Blood of stone : poems / by Tāriq Malik.
Names: Malik, Tāriq, 1951- author.
Identifiers: Canadiana 20230522319 | ISBN 9781773861265 (softcover)
Classification: LCC PS8626.A44 B56 2024 | DDC C811/.6—dc23

BLOOD OF STONE

poems

TĀRIQ MALIK

CAITLIN PRESS 2024

Contents

Kotli in the Middle Distance — Lahore   65

Locating Kotli Beyond — *ko-eth*   79

Foreword by Prabhjot Parmar

First introduced to Kotli Loharan—the ancestral home of Tāriq Malik—in his collection of short stories, *Rainsongs of Kotli* (2004), I was catapulted back to it in his book of poems *Exit Wounds* (2022). Speaking from his location in Canada as the "other," Malik, in his poems, had traversed geographies, including that of Kotli, to explore emotive themes emerging from myriad experiences as a native, as a refugee, as a migrant, and as a citizen. Traumatic moments—experienced or linked to the title *Exit Wounds*, led readers from the moment of rupture in 1947 when the colonial "kleptomaniacs" divided land and its people to the invasion of Kuwait in 1990, leading to Malik and his family's displacement. The poignancy of "Ammi-ji's Letter to Keshaliya" showcased his personal and collective loss as a result of partition; the visual memory of enemy bootprints in "The Home Invaded" and the tugging of heartstrings with a list of mundane yet irreplaceable things in "What We Lost During Our Third War" highlighted Malik's poetic prowess. The verbal and visual darkness on the page and the world in "Eidh in the Time of Covid" demonstrated his sensitivity to the immediate and the global.

At its heart, a sensorial feast, *Blood of Stone*, is a homage to Kotli Loharan. The spatial distance from home and temporal distance from personal and historical events melds into evocations of moments, people, structures, and events of Kotli and other geographies. A feature in *Exit Wounds*, the braiding of text and image in *Blood of Stone* also situates thematic elements such as home, memory, loss, friendship, love, and mobility alongside the sensory. Notwithstanding the sensorial distance and deprivation, the memory of smell underpins Malik's poetry. It emanates from the selected images of the homes and streets of Kotli included in the text. Engaging the olfactory, the man from the clan of the "last lohars" [blacksmiths] (*Exit Wounds*) becomes another artisan who deftly weaves the warp and weft of a thread of myriad colours and experiences to create a visual of weaving, of a tapestry to set in motion an immersive sensorial experience meticulously presented in three parts: Kotli in distance, mid-way, and Kotli beyond ko-eth.

For readers, particularly those from South Asia or the tropics, the pull into Malik's world begins with the smell of warm earth and rain in his preface photo essay, "kotli petrichor." If exhilarating moments of "kittu plots bo kaata!" and "raba raba meen barsa" capture the Punjabi ethos, then through the symbols of colour appearing in titles or in lines such as "the ochre of blossoms / the silver of the moon," Malik captivates the reader with his mastery over the visual. "Kotli Petrichor" is peppered with images of relics of a bygone era for which there is a considerable longing. Photographs of ruins and rubble serve as reminders of the past, but there is a life in which vines grow, and birds and insects find sustenance. The decaying architectural remnants have become nursery sites for non-human life that thrive without the threat of imminent violence and communal divides. Such symbolic metaphors elevate Malik's poetry to philosophical reflections rooted in the personal and the political.

Like *Exit Wounds*, Malik brings readers to motifs of portals that offer the possibility of opening or parting for passage and mobility (in "Shared Wall"). Or, "In-between the portals of History" reminds of restrictions, sealed fates, and histories of people waiting to be unlocked; for example, the image of a padlock securing an old wooden door in Kotli whose residents with centuries of lineage in its soil have not returned home since 1947. Similarly, the three poems in "Monopoly of Ink" offer a forceful critique of exclusionary practices in publishing.

Malik's poems capture the rural flavour that is often missing from poetry written in English, as most South Asian poets writing in English would be of urban origin. The rural idiom, the vocabulary that is either forgotten or seldom used thousands of miles away from Kotli, Pakistan, or India, would intrigue and delight readers. For instance, the translated short poems "Kujian: Earthen Bowls," "Pangurhe: The Cradle," and "Patolay / Ragdolls." South Asian readers, especially Punjabis, of a particular vintage would cherish the evocation of "takhati," "bo-kaata," and some of the other items rarely seen these days, especially in the diaspora in Canada. Others would be compelled to visualize the intimate, social, and communal conviviality. The beauty of Malik's poems lies in their accessibility for readers of any background, not just South Asian. Having taught *Exit Wounds* at different levels in university, I have observed first-hand student excitement as they engaged with his poems. I am confident that students and other readers will embrace *Blood of Stone* as enthusiastically. Its range and depth will (re)introduce readers to poems anchored in geography, history, and culture that reflect on past and present using sensorial, botanical, and ornithic imagery and, at times, photographs. *Blood of Stone* is, to borrow from Malik, "the spell of dream worlds / page by page."

Kotli Petrichor in the Far Distance

Introduction

Hidimibi: "I taught him smell. The odour of roe and rabbit,
of morel and toadstool, the distant hint of petrichor."

—Karthika Naïr, *Until the Lions: Echoes from the Mahabharata*

Petrichor (/'pɛtriˌkɔ:r/) is the earthy scent produced when rain falls on dry soil.
The word is constructed from Ancient Greek πέτρα (pétra) 'rock,' or πέτρος
(pétros) 'stone,' and ἰχώρ (ikhṓr), the ethereal fluid that is the blood
of the gods in Greek mythology.

In this follow-up to my previous poetry book, *Exit Wounds*, and my short story collection, *Rainsongs of Kotli*, I pick up the threads I had begun weaving into the Kotli narrative.

It takes a village to raise a child, and this book began as a love poem to one such village, Kotli Loharan, under the working title of Kotli Petrichor. Fortunately, I realized early on the difficulty first readers had with the titles of Kotli and Petrichor. I think renaming it to *Blood of Stone* captures my aspirational and poetic conceit and the inherent thrust of this narrative.

Kotli is located in the Pakistani northeastern Punjab, and unfortunately for its inhabitants, it lies very close to the Pakistan–India Kashmir border. This fact has meant

that the chaos of the Partition and the traumas of dislocation and migration are still part of the recent personal history of the inhabitants of this land. The pages dedicated to Shared Walls explore the spatial and temporal intersections of that historical violence in Kotli.

I come from a generation that knew better than to name their infants before their second year. This is why, whenever I came home from my boarding school, my aging maternal grandmother, my nanni, would say: *Come here, my precious babu, let me see you in the light by the window*. It was also the motivation for our older relatives, who lived so far that visiting them required a tanga ride, to begin hurling soft abuses at our parents as soon as they saw us entering their street. This was their way of showing us their love and concern for us and chiding our parents for having kept us apart from them for so long.

It has been such a long journey from their world of purdah, and the chadurs, dupattas, and shawls raised over their heads and only partly held open in front of the face like a radar pointing towards the mahram of the inner sanctum and away from the non-mahram.

My early life in Kotli abruptly ended when I was six, and attending a local school in the Urdu medium, when my family moved to Kuwait to join my father. After attending an Arabic school for another year, I was transferred to Burn Hall School, Abbottabad in Pakistan, an English boarding school. There, I was fortunate to have Father Johnson as my English teacher for the final five years.

I quickly learned that ever since his arrival in Punjab, our Father Johnson had been busy sabotaging "Macaulay's Mandate" of converting us into "Englishmen in manners and skills, but still brown in colour." As part of our high school curriculum, we spent five years learning, among other subjects, the social history of the Middle Ages town of Tankersham in central England so that at the end of these lessons, I could proudly describe in great detail the history, social conditions, and power structures established there.

One summer, before I set out on my holidays, Father Johnson assigned me a personal growth task: "When you get home, observe the seasonal crops for this time of the year.

Ask when is the harvest time? What seasonal celebrations are your folks preparing for? Bring these details to me. And find out where the Tawi ends."

I stared back at him in bewilderment. "What's Tawi?" I asked sheepishly.

"Go and find out."

Cloistered in Burn Hall, I knew everything and then some of the English town of Tankersham yet knew nothing of what was happening that day in backwater Kotli.

Though my eleven years of stay at Burn Hall were marked by acute homesickness, the final year was one of the proverbial rude awakening. I gradually began noticing the natural environment around me and taking notes. Decades later, these notes would find their way into my first book, *Rainsongs of Kotli*, and I owe more than that book to Fr. Johnson. My hometown of Kotli would eventually became my Mokondo, my Malgudi, and finally, my Tankersham.

In venturing across a river with no visible opposite shore, and having to cross the feared dark waters of *kaala paani*, the Kotli walahs were ever mindful to carry their Zamzam-soaked shrouds with them lest death overtake them and find them unprepared for proper burial. Wherever they fell, they all lie facing Makkah in the west, their bodies collapsed around their hearts, each the size of their fists, now in the company of their preceding generations. They lie beyond the reach of any generational griots who have also now fallen equally from relevance in an age that would rather perform a lobotomy on itself than recall its history.

Sometimes, they lie collapsed in the sands where they toiled, the caravans having marched on without them, and are buried in clusters so very close to each other, already one with their soaked shrouds, humbled by white cotton, loosely bound like the tunics for the Haj. And in the case of one troubled soul too beautiful for this world, Shafiq, the artist of radio wires, now lies all alone at the bottom of the shallow waters off the Arabian Gulf within an exploded, sunken vessel, the *MV Dara*.

Though my parents and I were born in the same village, *their* village was located in a different country, thanks to the whims of the entitled grifters camped inside our nation's doors. In the two centuries following our colonization, we would only escape the blast furnace of Raj's kleptocracy by scattering as collateral damage across the continents. Some headed for the Middle East, others to the east coast of Africa. Epitomizing the desperation of those early generations, an uncle, Babaji Feroze, would set out for Panama in search of employment, settle briefly in England before retreating to Kotli.

However, wherever they chose to settle, coming to the end of their stay, the tug of genetic memory would lead them to seek out the taste of their place of birth, and, like returning salmon, they would be delivered back home, broken in body and spirit, their sweat having nurtured infertile soils of thankless and churlish peoples. Their self-sacrifice was heroic in its aspiration to fling us as far as possible from the shuttered workshops and locked doors of Kotli. This book borrows from their lived experiences.

On these pages, besides my close family, we encounter a world inhabited by other characters from their generation. We meet Mohammad Din - kulfi walah, setting out at dawn, lured by the city with its promise of shiny lights and soiled coins; here is an aunt of fortunes whose personal misfortune had delivered her into our lives. Here is Kittu, my seven-year-old alter-ego, making a comeback in pursuit of his obsession with kite flying, and also and a passing reference to my first big crush. A desert jerboa makes a brief appearance in seeking companionship.

Note: Wherever the reader encounters the word *ko-eth*, the colloquial Punjabi pronounce; please substitute it with the term 'the chickenshit planet of kuwait.' I want to stay faithful in recording my family's legacy (three generations and counting) of slaving in this meat grinder for over seven decades.

mohammed din — kulfi-walah

in summer

the first ritual involves his wife / churning boiling milk
  adding cardamom flavour / rooh afza essence / pistachio almond texture
    while he chips the ice block / packs the array of 136 ice-cream pockets
      & by dawn his giant frame folding on itself
        rough hands clutching flimsy handles
          the kulfi cart rattling in the dark
            the lit city with its shiny coins only 7 miles away
              then before dusk he heads homewards
            the nearly empty cart / tipsy on darkened road
          entering the village / he is beset upon by street urchins
        who demand *kulfi kulfi ifluk kulfi*
      but mohammed din – kulfi-walah / brushes them all aside
    until his return step alerts his children / who swarm around him
  for them he scoops out the soggy leftovers

silently

mohammed din — sabzi-walah

in winter

this second ritual involves whatever is in season
   potatoes bitter gourd pumpkin spinach
      before each dawn his giant frame folds on itself
         wrapping the chadar tight around his shoulders
           rough hands clutching the flimsy handles
             the vegetable cart rattling in the dark
               the lit city with its shiny coins only 7 miles away
                  then before dusk he heads homewards
            the nearly empty cart / tipsy on the darkened road
          entering the village / he is beset upon by street urchins
       who demand *kulfi kulfi kulfi* / but mohammed din – sabzi-walah
     is too tired to protest / *who buys kulfi ifluk kulfi in winter*
   until his return step alerts his children / who swarm around him
for them he scoops up leftover leafy grits

silently

in the fall

this is the grist of the life & times of a mohajir giant feeding a family of six
        until felled at 37 in mid-step
             on the road to the lit city of shiny coin
                felled a mile short of home
                   in the grip of deep freeze
                      a lone nightwatchman rattles his stick for company
                        comes to the end of his rounds
                              spetstoof sih secarter
                    over mute rutted
                    centuries-old cobblestones
                    his retreat marked by a nightbird's call
                    hedgehogs scuttling underground
                    frost crunching underfoot

                  silence
                  descending

weaving spiderwebs over open wounds

the ambulance careens into spilled sunlight
with the restraining bunkbed cold as the slab
on which a coroner examined your body
minutely
for the worth of a life

you taught yourself early
to weave spiderwebs over open wounds
soothed our aches with mantras
nim leaves are bitter but heal
& five times daily
guided every blossom in prayer
to seek the illusive ka'bah
behind every distant horizon

then late into this fracturing
you believe each week a day
closer to our visit
& yet somehow through the cobwebs
you are mindful not to ask too much
our long absences
the short distances separating
as you fill the spaces in-between
with generations hence
their flung open arms
your lap heavy
with squirming drooling grandchildren

while you feed us childhood favourites
      gajar da halwa   missi roti   saag
      & cooling in a water tub
          ripe mangoes   watermelons
      & under an inverted basket
          a live chicken   awaiting fate
for baba-ji   already a decade gone
      you stoke the hookah
      hang out his starched turban
& if you notice the setting sun
      you hug us even closer
          willing nightfall to suspension

winding our way through desolation
      the ambulance lurches onto cemetery floor
we wring our hearts
      to wilt the sun
while your every blossom tracks
      the perpetually receding ka'bah

by day's end   a centaur

spurred homewards
bright tassels & plumes
ragged yoke bindings
each has withstood another journey
the carriage unyoked
abandoned for the night
the rider now holds the reins loosely
even letting them trail on the ground
trusting that the charge that led him
all the way to the city & back
across this lifetime
is not going to drift far

both equally spent
half asleep
need something
to hold onto

a loose horseshoe rattles
across the path
sparks flying in the dark
a passerby sees fireflies
amongst the gravestones

by midnight
a stallion this side of the night
a human that side of the day
with every leap
a centaur traversing the sky
dislodges stars

ablutions before surrendering the body

who else but *you*
for the final ablutions by the eldest son
        this most challenging is also the most revered
whoever heard of a son refusing to wash his father's body
        even the prophets took it upon themselves

i protest
        i am too young
        not even a man
        not yet ready for this
        i am only two hands
        one body
        no mind

much later
there comes a moment
when we must offer a shoulder one final time
        & though there is nothing left of you
                the load is heavy
                        it scrapes my bones
                until we lower you right here
                        by this pomegranate
                        that you once planted
        to which i will add
                gulmohar for colour
                motia for aroma
                night blooming chambeli
& we lower you right here
        gently gently gently
                back into the scent of fresh uprootings

someone once snatched you from this spot
        & raked & churned this dust
        shook you awake
        set you upright

allotted you a paltry span
      of days to weave this sunlight
      nights pondering stars
      contemplating self
        & progeny
      shading saplings from sun
      watering roots

when i turn back to look
      at the mound of fresh earth
you are already sitting up
mumbling
      beta
    do you hear me
    i am not ready for any of this
    i am only a man
    no hands
    no body
    no mind
      do you hear me

yet i head back for the empty home
      to bide my time till nightfall
when i return to dig
      & you place your hand firmly
        on my aching shoulder
          whispering
          chalo

    only now
there is a day-old gash in the ground
      of human length & breadth
        earth awaiting its overdue balance

maassi paagan — my aunt of fortunes

Maassi Paagan settled with her surviving mohajir family members in our vacated
neighbouring house after the troubles of the Partition. I only knew her as a caring, tragic
and quiet presence in my early life as an aya. I learned much later that her husband had
been killed during the journey that brought her to Kotli.
Here, she reflects on her loss.

you once reassured me
      every river delivers an opposite shore

this river in flood   had none
      offering only mouthfuls of barbed wire
      & borders pelted by rain
& only the water   brimming
      drifting beyond our clasped bodies

the water was relocating tree trunks
      bigger than our hut
redistributing our fields
      erasing banks
reworking the map of our villages
      & gouging its mind   as well as ours
soon our past lives together would also be a memory
here only human sighing
      would end the night

how could i have remained sane
      & stood in its way

it was not only the river that took you from me
      but human hands
      performing the final rituals
my wrenched insides
      splayed across the riverbank
my beloved
      i wanted to stay

but the water would not stop
        brimming
the same waters that carried you
        to that unseen shore
bore me here
        bathed in fresh soil
this glistening shore
        its skin scrubbed clean with blood

i do not belong here
        amongst these dead & dying
with you now living on a separate street
        that does not intersect
& me with just this one life
        & that one now not easy to surrender

yet every moment i drift closer to you
        rest well & wait

here is a measure of sanity
        comfort in anonymity & quiet domesticity
yet each day i wait for that moment
even if time here is opaque
        sluggish as river mud
        while your shore rapidly recedes

my father holding a butcher's knife over my crib

how many of us across the global embrace
      in shared simulacra of the qurbani
have woken to the sight
      of our fathers holding a butcher's knife
          over our cribs
    beta
touch this knife for blessing
    a sacrifice must be made
then the queasy return to sleep
underneath the new eidh costume
      hung spotless on the wall
while the blood letting
      shielded from your view
          arrays glistening body parts
          mutely across verandah
          eyes milking over dull
& you awaken
      to the offering of liver still quivering warm
          trimmed of fat
          skewered flavoured roasted

often
      dusting myself awake
      from a retreating carnival of youth
          i return to the moment
when a hand awakens me
    beta...

this is how a trickle of rust
      encounters baked brick
      overwhelms the gutters

how unbearable the weight of a devotee's tears

for Kashmiri-American poet, Agha Shahid Ali

lime green

at the mausoleum of *pir sabz*
the faithful congregate   at this   their first annual *urs*
revelling   in the many splendoured deeds
of their benefactor
donning his eponymous   lime green garments

the shroud & tomb are perched precariously
between   cliff edge   ravenous river
last year's flood   claimed boundary wall
this year   mere faith & tradition
retain in place   what remains
keeping hungry waters   at bay

heading homewards at dusk
cocooned   in afterglow of adorations
blessed   with fresh rounds of ganja
the pilgrims celebrate
how for them   in each quotidian gesture
miracles   now   await
how   even the undersides of monsoon clouds
reflect   the lime green of rice paddies

the devotees   weep

ochre red

a lifetime & a continent away
a poet watches an approaching dust storm
pouring volcanic ochre
onto his pristine snow shrouded mountains & vale
musing to himself
this is the blood of hassan   &   hussein
the soil of karbala   gifted to us soiled
here   in distant kashmir

the devotee in him   weeps

i watch daily my life erased under gaachni

all it takes to erase the day's toil
        is a ritual dunking under water pump
& the relief of rubbing the day's lessons out of sight
        then
applying a fresh grey skin of gaachni paste
        rebirthing   refreshing   relieving
            in every coat of slate

at any moment after school   a dozen of us
        are seen waving our wooden takhti tablets in air
        chiming our relief to the wind
& in our skilled hands
        the cane pen tip is sharpened   slotted
            cut diagonally   *just so*

when all our yesterdays
        are eventually judged & put to sleep
the body will still keep its score
        the schoolmaster's cane
        his favourite student's pummelling
        our peer's verbal licks
            as we sit on our haunches
            pinched earlobes
            serving penance

the body will keep its score
        how all our raw un-adult-erated glee
            was beaten out of us

we were

      doctors   engineers   chefs   lovers   singers

      even   poets in-waiting

impatient to uncover   the written   in stars

      but all our words were knocked

            out of our lips

            & our pen nibs

   so   *so*   *very*   *early*

   now there is no more skin left

underneath these layers of gaachni

   only this unheal of scars

raba raba meen barsa

This is how the season of rainbirds summons the harbingers of *saun padron*

here the fishermen croon   of the *mitha sup*
       the sweet poisonless bite of snake
that will allow them to reap the river harvest

          raba raba meen barsa
          saade jaal vich machhi pa

& our children   who pluck the baya's woven nests
       to use as slippers
in every step   hatchlings tweet

          raba raba meen barsa
          saade peri juthi pa

& in the flooded fields
the transplanted rice seedlings   pray

          raba raba meen barsa
          saadi khethi danay pa

& the well frogs   croak
amidst their circle of soak of bricks

          raba raba meen barsa
          saade khu vich paani pa

& not to be outdone
the frosted storks   playing footsie with leeches
daintily pick out catfish   & pray

          raba raba meen barsa
          saadi khethi dhadhu pa

kittu plots bo kaata!

"Bo kaata" is the Punjabi expression of triumph upon slicing through your opponent's kite thread

the first declaration of the season of basant
       a stack of tattered kites   freshly restored
          & spot plastered with aloe vera
      hoarded under charpai
      guarded in sleep
while we watch the silent sleep of the threaded manifold
      within the death grip of its coils
& through it all
how unsilent sleeps kittu   mumbling
      to crisscrossed skies
      to creatures of whisp
      sheer glue ricepaper thread
& in his restive dreams
he confronts such mysteries
      the way thorns of a dead kikar tree
          reach out to snare your favourite kites
      the way clay marbles only skim their targets

the errant fall of a cut twig
        in the whack of gulli-dhandha
the way a taped tennis ball englishes a whisper
        from the willow of cricket bat
& why hedgehogs scuttle
        across his path on moonlit nights
why the ripest jaman
        are always lodged out of reach
why coins hurled from the wedding parades
        always roll into the gutters
why there is never enough weight in his pockets
why the price of every carnival joyride
        is always beyond his height

he is exhausted
he waited an entire nine months for just the right shards
        sheer blue
        ground to finest spice
        filtered through finest muslin
        then glued to finest kite thread

        the one with the image of the fairy
        only *pari marka* will do   *lethal*

it took all of yesterday
        & a simmering pot of glass glue dye string
        in hands stained   a royal sky blue
where the precise amount of ground glass
        has been central to this affair
                too much & it will slit its own wrists
                too little & others will slit its throat
this war can only be won
        by strategizing such vital details

now watch how kittu ventures out   onto blistering rooftop
& flattens the stretched fabric across his oily hair
& twirls threaded manifold
   fine tunes its musical registers
   conjures new taunts for his opponents

the kite   once set free
a jinn against the noon sky sizzle
   nicks crooked fingers
   burns through palms
   slices every other kite thread
a lifetime of such basant afternoons is to follow
& he revels in his rooftop wiles
   this slick lifeline disappearing
     into the receding folds
     of Allah kareem's blue beard
   where the glue of sky
   suspends this wilful creature
     mere stick & rice paper

when an errant wind
   tumbles the kite back onto blistering rooftop
   its spine shattered
     paper body tattered
how promptly   does rooftop surgery restore
   aloe vera glue patching wounds
& the kite still safe from other grubby hands
   soaring again
   wobbly   but airworthy
kittu's wild untamed bird
   its heart still beating wild free
   blending into blue

basant o basant
      basant of the young   & the poor
& how this *must* be heaven for any seven-year-old
        whose life purpose is rooftop battle
        until the ground shard cleaves
            until rings the cry
              bo kaata   bo kaata

a cry kittu has hoarded in his throat all through parched summer

      a cry he has yet to utter

my first big crush

When Balqees leans into you, you stay leaned into

saanji deevaar (shared wall)

Artist statement: In-between the Portals of History

Kotli Loharan, my Punjabi hometown, is near the border between Northern-western India and North-eastern Pakistan. During the bloody Partition of colonial India along religious lines by the British in mid-August 1947, several million inhabitants were massacred in this region; over twelve million were forced to relocate across the newly established borders. The Partition was marked by a complete administrative failure of the British Raj and also by the lack of any culpability by the perpetrators for this tragedy of ethnic cleansing. The year 2022 marked the seventy-fifth anniversary of this immense human tragedy.

My poetry and the art pieces on the following pages locate this historical chaos between two locked doorways. The contained space glimpsed through opposite-facing doors—one permitting a limited entry and the other denying exit. This turmoil is symbolized by the montage of images of physical destruction, a space of limbo where both adversaries are still unable to resolve their mutual historical traumas and thus unable to imagine or embrace a future of peaceful co-existence.

in-between the portals of history

(Please read/listen to these instructions carefully)

ESCAPE ~~EXIT~~ ENTRY

(Located @ Kotli, West Punjab, Pakistan)
~~Kharooj~~ Dakhool / ~~Egress~~ Ingress
~~Denied~~ ONLY Permitted on 14-Aug-1947
Disclaimer: *~~Exit~~ Enter At Your Own Risk*
(Absolutely NO Shortcuts Permitted)

Until further notice: Entry is only ~~denied~~ permitted after 12:00 a.m.

Escape Clause: Watch out for flashing lights

(Please read/listen to these instructions carefully)

ENTRY ~~ESCAPE~~ EXIT
(Located @ Gurdaspur, East Punjab, India)
~~**Dakhool**~~ **Kharooj / ~~Ingress~~ Egress**
~~**Permitted**~~ **Denied till 15-Aug-2022**
Disclaimer: *~~Enter~~ Exit At Your Own Risk*
(Absolutely NO Shortcuts Permitted)

Until further notice: Egress is now ~~permitted~~ denied after 12:00 a.m.

Escape Clause: Due to budget constraints
the flashing lights at the end of the tunnel have been switched off

the alchemy of a house composing itself

we were long gone   elsewhere
long before the conflagrations
oil lamps flaring   hissing
fueled by wayward moths   chirping
meeting their conclusions   enflamed
while wayward   we
absconded   fattened
ripening in our youth
the house always greeted us back
with sooty face   crumbling walls
accusing only in its graffitied grime
the narrow hand-plied walls
once marching soldiers
now slipping out of formation
stretching their legs easing their burden
tumbling   road hazards
you are loved   you are loved
you are loved in spite of yourself
while through your walls
move your benighted parents
blessing each detail of your lives
with unrequited attention
singing childhood hymns
sprinkling mumbled inexact prayers
circling the five daily ablutions
while the house slinks to dust
much later
someone will lift the carpet edge of day
uncover remnants
nights of lingering hunger

our backrooms remained cool through midsummer heat

through punjabi midsummer heat   our backrooms remained cool   but forbidden
unlit   reeking   spiced   mango pickled   amla   maraba-ed
long ago a buffalo would have been tethered here   lowing low when hungry
rattling chain to be milked   the creature had been rendered long ago
when i came along   the floor still reeked of her presence
the front room was framed high   out of reach   with room length shelving
laden   with our best brass utensils   & a persian glass hookah
that a grandparent brought home from abroad here abroad existed only in its artefacts
a large wooden gramophone box its original purpose lost now only stuff of family legends
a solar cap   the type the angrez wore   in faded daguerreotypes
the one our parents used to fetch   sand-fried popcorn   from the tandoor
two pairs of circular prescription glasses   wired together   which I inherited
& in a high corniche of one wall   the five books we owned
three copies of the work in a language the adults could read but *not* fully understand
fourth and fifth   a biography   & a commentary   on the first three
the final   the only one they could understand   &   quote to us
decades later   the house continued to smell of buffalo   though it had
been consumed long since the   chain   rattling

still-life with peripatetic

for Abaid and Khalid Mughal

anchored by boulders of parents
our two-storey home held its head in the clouds
    roots digging deep
    allowing us safe passage
        in skipping across rooftops

where we skinned our knees
    racing up & down those steep staircases
leaping too recklessly in pursuit of stray kites
leaning too precariously on crumbling bannisters

here we sought & always found
    footholds across the grime
embrace of our every dare
    a nest of wild parrots
    a menace of wasp nests
    a peek into the next-door witch's lair

    eventually
other lives would expose our innocence
revealing that what held each brick in place
was foreknowledge
    the anchoring boulders
    were already tiring to tumble

& with the fathers gone
we too would abandon our mothers
        to the shawls of their grief
to dwell within leaky adobes
at the mercy of local wolves
having put lifetimes oceans continents
between them & our high-rises
with our offspring embarrassed
        by an alien mother tongue

oceans apart from siblings
        the missing sons overseas
        the departed daughters at their in-laws
far from progeny
        one such mother would spend her final afternoons
perched at the foot of her street
        on a neighbour's doorstep
where she engaged with an indifferent world
        in the vicarious comings & goings
        of other people's great grandchildren
        wealth prosperity success
            all locked in a daze

if you live long enough
parents husband children friends
        are all claimed one by one
while mold smothers
        every feature of a once familiar world

a hushed field awaits the monsoon

slaked dew
crosshatches the moon
god's patchwork of flooding fields
even the trilling crickets
amidst settling dews
resound with the bullfrogs
& how sudden is the realization
that while you sat & chatted
the field has been drenched in dew
drawing our attention upwards
where arrayed enormities beam their final gasps

how little of the light you really need
in the barest wisp of october crescent
to survive the dark
washing into dawn

the grass blades rustle
a cool breeze sieves the grass
i've been away too long

how long was this lying in wait
the clover snapping back into shape
the frenetic crickets silenced
slaked

a sketch of someone who may not be in the scene

This remarkable, faded 1945 (pre-Indian Partition) monotone, an enlargement of a much smaller image, was reprinted to locate the last traces of a young family member who died prematurely. My Babaji's fifth son, Ghafoor, was the last son to pass away in Babaji's lifetime. Somewhere in the hectic chaos of this frame of an uncle's wedding portrait may be Ghafoor's last known visage.

Our family's obsession with periodically scouring this image for traces of Ghafoor has yet to reliably identify him amongst the fifty-odd guests recorded here. Now that all the eyes that once so lovingly beheld him are finally all asleep, I often scan the image to see if time will reveal any new revelations from it.

In the upper left corner, I can identify the head of the mare on which the bridegroom is perched. In the foreground are eight wedding band musicians, each probably sounding off simultaneously on their individual instruments. In this cacophony of music, ambient sounds, and the sea of faces, Ghafoor, my cousin, would probably have seen the photographer, and knowing that stillness is required for this moment to be captured for posterity, he must stand still. That is my hope for the past.

Perhaps technology at the time expected too much of an eleven-year-old to be motionless for the precious few moments required for this image to gel. Perhaps future technology will improve sufficiently upon the resolution and undo the blurred parts; perhaps AI will eventually figure out how to undo the ravages of time on a much scanned and enlarged image of an image.

Or, perhaps, our fervent speculation will all have been in vain, and the subject had never been in the frame.

as the bodies settle in

insomniac restless
they suffer from various degrees of
restless leg syndromes brain fogs clouded in cobwebs
tending to linger over the unfinished

caught in mid-step retreat
roots nudge bricks out of alignment
       and a graveyard wall collapses
             detonating the gate
at every swish of our footfall
       earthen mound   to   earthen mound
       weeds smother hammered trails
memory slips   overflows
our every measured step watered with tears

though we tread lightly
the earth pushes back each blade we trample
      each leaf   mulch for a shared past
      every airborne fruit   reclaiming earth

buddha bowl

the light hesitant footfall of a fakir at your doorstep
    is always a blessing
    and households that feed the fakir
        will also feed stray dogs that accompany him

as i cautiously tread my way from one household to next
    on both sides of the lohars' street
        the sunlit & the shaded
the offerings are often from the hands of shrouded figures
    always given in modesty
    eyes averted
or from the hands of children who have been instructed
    do not linger at the door

today the mirzas are offering leftover biryani
my bounty from the mughal household
   is a multi-hued khichri for the bowl
the awans may have a piping hot roti

the sufi at our shrine has taught us
   always be generous
   the stranger at your door
   maybe the angel jibraeel in disguise

but mostly my call goes unanswered
   and today my begging bowl garners
     only indifference

the degs of miraj sharif

their urgent message awoke me early
>the *mirasi* brothers *sakhiya & mukhya*
the drummers have been frenetic
>even this late into the afternoon
>each still possessed by the message
and now the whole village knows
today is the holiest of holy *miraj sharif*
>and this day brings blessings for all

>my mouth is already watering

long before the giant *degs* arrive
>each capacious enough to contain me
someone is already knocking bricks together
>and setting up makeshift fireplaces
i hear their heaves as each *deg*
>is rolled edge over edge
>>and lifted in place

today there are to be three
>two *degs* for the pulao
>and one for the sweet rice *zarda*

as the afternoon wanes
the rice simmers sizzles splatters
>under the churning swish of scrapers
this late in the day
the *degs* have now been set aside to stew
>their clay lids sealed with flour
i can hear the hiss of their garland of coals

much later
when the feast is finally ready
>and the prayers dispensed with
>the solicitations made
>the saints appeased
the *degs* are unsealed

& over the lure of browned onions
  wafts the aroma of *rooh kewra*
  saffron cardamom rosewater
smaller pots are now filled
  to be rushed to the supplicant's household
the next dishfuls are for their relatives
& then for the lazy fat ones
  the lean ones
  the hangers-on
  the sycophants
  the dervishes
  the maimed

until
  for us the blind
what remains
  is the best of all
  the caramelized *krori*
  rice scraped directly off the bottom

the drums fall silent
  the *degs* rolled away
  in reverse edge over edge
i hear dogs sniff at the smouldering coals
  while i dream of the next blessed
  day of *miraj sharif*

a lamentation for mute horses

Translations from the Punjabi Poetry of Laeeq Babri

Ghughu Kohre: From the original Punjabi text with permission from Dr. Laeeq Babri, at the University of the Punjab, Lahore, 1974.

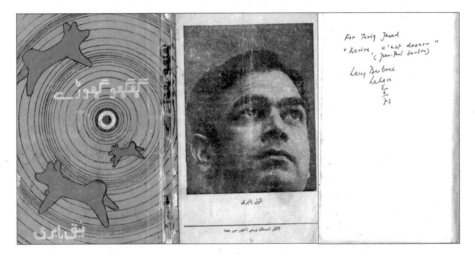

The cover of Laeeq Babri's Ghughu Kohre (1971, Lahore) & a personal message on the first page

Piglay Saye: Molten Shadows

Who set ajar
      these windows
      these doors
unravelling
      the spell of dream worlds
      page by page

Ghaat Di Dhoban: The Ghat Washerwoman

O waters of futility
      into you I squander my fate
O barren fields
      with you I align my fortune

Kujian: Earthen Bowls

It is in these that the blameless potter's wife
        seeks recompense
blessing each spring leaf
          for its day of toil
and with what futility she spreads
          her earthen bowls to dry
while monsoons taunt
        beckon

Pangurhe: The Cradle

Now that the monsoon holds sway
over the perpetual innocence of the cradle
        our unrequited yearnings
            flutter in the wind
and in the flurry of words
       all misgivings are laid bare
coming to rest
       by the unyielding walls

The guests of desire
       scrape the mud from their boots
          depart
Yet
the carnival of innocence
       holds sway over the crib
and bestows upon a scorched earth
       rumours of monsoons yet to come

Dholi: The Bridal Palanquin

Stepping into her bridal palanquin did Heer cry out to her companions
— Waris Shah, *Heer*

Who is not familiar
with the season of farewells
     and how past discretions
    will often drift by
       uncelebrated
and how the remorseless
    bid farewell
   to the night
      shying from its milky whiteness

In the bridal palanquin
no companion recognizes
    the scars bestowed
    by past indiscretions

Patolay: Ragdolls

How else to recall
the lingering dusk
    slithering into the gaps
    between words
where all our forlorn ragdolls
    lie in tatters
the only witnesses
    to such thievery

In turning to the day's companions
    nowhere do we find
    our forgotten lullabies

to the *daktars* who stitch leaves & birdsongs onto trees

i guide her through a darkened corridor
     of bandaged heads
this
     the final step in my mother's return
     to face normal light without shades

exiting
     she is astonished by the exuberant foliage before her
        tak   look
     she exclaims excitedly
       the daktar has put leaves onto the trees

     sometimes at dusk
her son heads for a secluded stand of trees
     & pumps up the volume
        on his state of the art hearing aids
& is startled by the symphony of birds
        bathing the forest

blessed are the ophthalmologists that bring the foliage back
blessed are the audiologists that amplify birdsong

ablur

How I dearly miss my friend, Ihsan Piracha (1952 – 2018)

Ihsan Piracha (R) in Abbottabad, Pakistan (1969)

the only image i have of you smiling
is when you step out

of the frame, in the next one
you are distracted, ablur

the only image i have of you smiling
is when you look up suddenly

moving too fast for the pixels
to gel you register in nuances,

fidget, or blink rapidly
before i realize

we could be at this
a lifetime & not miss a beat

the only image i have of you smiling
is off camera

stand still for once
dammit

we'll always be here for you

for my brother, Arif Javed

somewhere on the way to …
something caught *your* eye
and *you* pulled over
hoisting the bike onto its stand
and stood transfixed by the roadside
wondering
… now
how did they do that
pasting that silver balloon
so high on the faded horizon
someone tall had an even taller ladder handy
while several someones held its base
and steadied the person climbing
tricking him into trusting his own instinct
shouting
go high higher higher
we'll always be here for you

all the while
passers-by continued their drive-by
unmoved
as if this was the most common thing to see
a helium birthday balloon tacked to a distant horizon
there was after all
nothing extraordinary
about a moon anchored to its heaven
it occurs most nights

meanwhile
the long-suffering roadside sarson field
continued blooming
filling the air with its maddening aroma
you even saw a farmer peek out from his hut
to see what the fuss was all about
and returned to bed
muttering to his wife
not enough light to harvest
the rush of road
the ochre of blossoms
the silver of moon
the whisper of breeze
… not enough light to harvest
the toil of day still ahead
meanwhile
you stood by this same roadside
arms-folded

stunned to silence

the desperation of gleaners

death stalks   every out of reach mouthful
the desperation of gleaners   sweeping
the length & breadth of the field   repeatedly
the adults harvesting the stalks   crushed underfoot
the hungrier infants following   closer to ground
gleaning what the adults   miss
         both hands popping the grain   into mouths

when the field is abandoned   by humans
         others   move in

far from the field
headcloths   become sieves
the bounty   redistributed

later   ever mindful of tomorrows
         they wrench out their last mouthful
         fling it to the wind

rainsong in malhaar

for my Nina

the *sapera* has a cure for the cobra's bite
and an antidote for the scorpion's sting
and the *hakeem* a balm for every physical wound
the *sufi* an amulet for kali's evil eye
hadija can cast a *mantar*
over wayward husband
bored housewife
and even offer a cure for the *churail's* spell
or a possession by the *jinn*

but there is no escape
for the one smitten
by the sidelong glance of the beloved
from the arch of her brow
no one heals

Kotli in the Middle Distance — Lahore

the whole world is a masjid

it was time for noon prayer
& only this one room available
the only furnishings   a sturdy table & one chair
& the floor flooded

there is a guiding injunction for such situations

pray anywhere
the whole world is a masjid

& ever mindful
of the allotted timeframes for prayer
their actions were measured & deliberate
relying on a lifetime of such rituals

the photographer's eye

triggered by the novelty of the gelling image
had no such instructions to rely on
other than being mindful of allotted timeframes
he worked fast while composing

a lifetime of observing light
triangulating prisms
analyzing geometrics of shadows
configuring the low lying ceiling
the elevated positioning of his subjects

composing off-centre

snap

why we decided to leave his cellphone on

…since none of those left behind
were ready just yet to let him go
       the decision was unanimous

& now there is this busy signal over the line
i can sense someone at the other end
       busy typing a response

       hurry
the portal may close any minute now
this may well be all we have
       of his final message

Rafi — sublime in five inflections

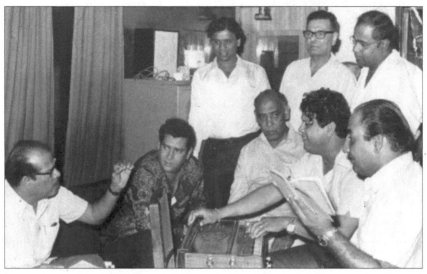

Manna Dey, Shammi Kapoor, Jaikishan, & Mohammed Rafi, during song rehearsal

once satisfied with their pooled inspirations
  the trio of lyricist composer musician
  gift their perfection
  into the hands of
    a chubby middle-aged
    unassuming balding male
    with a paunch
  to be the poster boy for their song

the evergreen & youthful voice
  first rehearses on a harmonium
    resting on a wooden chair
    a microphone hung low
the rapt audience allowing some breathing room
  as he disentangles the penultimate verse

*avaaz **mein** na dhoonga*
*avaaz mein **naa** dhoonga*
*avaaz mein na **dhoonga***
*avaaz mein na **dhoo-oonga***
***avaaaz** mein na dhoo-oonga*

dhun pahadhi
sublime in five inflections
fading to mute

world famous author frees street captives

*Journalist Amna R. Ali's photograph of South African novelist and playwright
Damon Galgut, Booker Prize winner, at the Lahore Literary Festival 2023*

the image deserved better headlines
& to his credit
seeing the captive beating wings
the writer does not ask of the street vendor   *why*
only *how much for two*
compelled to do something   *anything*
even if performative

he then carries the released captives before him
held close to breast
spiked false nipples
feeling their hearts racing
faster than the pulse in his fingers

suddenly embarrassed by their intimacy
a panic sets in   as he realizes

he may yet give them heart attacks
& so he tosses the throbbing creatures
seeding the sky

in a chaos of wings
they are gone
& he is taken aback
by their pulse   lingering
their warmth still disturbing the air

ah
he muses   *stepping gingerly onto the pavement*
if only flight could be won   so cheaply
& salvation gained   at no personal cost
where else   where else
purchase such easy miracles
on a playwriter's paltry savings
where else salvation   so close at hand

& now a darker shadow nibbles away his euphoria

how soon had the seller noticed
his vulnerability as a mark

— at first sight?
seared vision   a fish out of water?
clipped wings   the exposed skin?

with the victim safely out of sight
the seller heads into the bushes
retrieves his merchandise of clipped wings
amused
how soon without fail   the ones they set free
return to him   of their own volition

the safety of his net
comfort of their flock

a man possessed by his jinns

(Based on the Punjabi poet Munir Niazi's reading at Government College, Lahore, 1972)

the poet aflame is at best a whirling dervish
        who has forgotten his way home
        & stumbling across the world's stages
        spews contagion

my alma mater
after being pointedly asked by their exhausted sponsors
        when all the poets & artists
        desert their hometowns
        whose voice will still echo in the wind?
has finally reconsidered
& recalled its favourite son
the audience has come a long way
over three hundred are in attendance
        witnesses to this fit of nervous expiation
        & literary oversight

at the event
no words have so far been expressed
        for the poet is deep in stupor onstage
        & cannot be roused
& as he is being helped off the stage
        the gossip bleeds into whispers
        if the poet is a radio that is always on
            this one is fused

an inner cue suddenly triggers the poet
& he rises unsteadily
        holding up an index finger
        as if fine tuning into his personal wavelength

he begins inaudibly at first
>*kuj unj vee…*
>>several moments of silence follow
>*kuj unj vee raawan okhiyan san…*
>>the speech slurred
>*kuj ghal vich gham da tauk vi si*

in the hush that falls over the listeners
>the hesitant trickle now becomes a waterfall

>*when our paths were tortuous*
>*i carried forbearance for grief*
>>*when the town folk were sadistic*
>>*i nurtured a death wish*

sweeping lahore, 1972

swaddled in shawls
the sweepers peel themselves
  one by one
  from early morning monotone
& begin twirling their brooms
  sweeping in unison
  swish swish swish

where edge of pavement meets tarmac
  dust clouds filter the sun

a pair of morning sparrows
  preen night's ruffled feathers
  rise from my dorm windowsill
  compelled by distant grains
a dry twig snaps onto sidewalk
early morning traffic snarls
  slashing an ebbing tide of silence

stray dogs rise from gutters
  yawn scratch stagger
  set out in search of mercy or neglect

on the sheltered porch steps of our hostel
  one inert figure does not stir

homage to a purloined library

after the nine months of a wartime home invasion
i returned to ko-eth to discover all my books littering the floor
      their spines snapped

since then i have taken comfort
      in the memory of growing up
with the scriptures in my childhood home
      where no one slept or lay down
      with their feet pointing at the plinth
      on which rested the embroidered quran
& though this may have made
      for some awkward positioning of beds
the inhabitants mostly slept securely
      in the comfort of their conformity & reverence

writer annie dillard notes in her seminal *for the time being*
how scholars reading or studying the torah
      would place a cloth to cover it when finished
thus never leaving it open   when unattended

i am also mindful of writer karthika nair
noting that the *mahabharata*
being a fiery & dangerous book
      may even be fatal to read
      from beginning to end in linear sequence
& is not expected to be kept in the house
      lest it burn down

if only my humble ko-ethi purloined library
      had been held in such reverence

sumptuous ersatz of magyar posta

sumptuous   the philatelia
of ersatz magyar posta
      triangulate daguerreotype
      three inch rectangle
      some were even prismoid
celebrating one dictator or another
      in the breeze of fluttering flags
the parade of state machinery
      the march of the masses

within the boarding school carceral
      we had a habit of taking everything at its face value
& the grandiose propagandist fare
      from the continent of magyar
      in its shameless declaratives
      smothered in trademark declensions
dominated our bidding wars
did everything to feed our hunger
      but scream the reality
      stale goulash   cheap unicum

the one stamp that stood out for us all
      a metal sphere orbiting the earth
      its heartbeat a blip on our adoring radars
traded for four helveticas
      six of 10p GB
      & a whopping 12   *if pristine/uncancelled*

how could such beauty & care be lavished
      on a mere object designed
      only to soar upper right of a tiny oblong space
      the missives marching across various borders
      to reach our punjabi post office

& for decades we lived in the immediate fear
that the magyar philatelic designer
   the hero we had cast as a neglected cog
   in the bureaucratic warrens of his state
   toiling silently on his solitary passion
   lest his creativity come to notice
would be re-assigned elsewhere
even as we continued our desperate search
   to locate a pen pal
   on the generous continent of magyar

five decades later i am still searching
   still hoarding the six of 10p GB i traded

Locating Kotli Beyond — *ko-eth*

a desert jerboa seeks companionship

i

... the premature death of a young parent launches their offspring onto unforeseen tangents / mine was to do two decades of time in the desert / where i perfected the art of banging my numbed head against a wall / until relief would be offered / only when i stopped /

ii

... how / during night shifts the body keeps its score /

... so that when i shuffle the pages of a biography at work / was it a coincidence that the chemical plant was located next to a biscuit factory / whose early morning aroma of fresh baking / drove us mad at the end of our shifts /

... or that the brittle-candy factory stood adjacent to an spca facility / processing orphaned furry little creatures till dawn / its chimney choked with drifting fumes / & the stench heavy with burnt flesh /

... mercifully / the pillow & quilt factory for stuffing down / was nowhere near the goose farm /

iii

... how alone / during endless nightshifts on the ground floor of a factory churning salines / i learned to roar with the 'lions' till i was hoarse / the whining shoulder-high pumps that swirled a million gallons / of chemical shit /

... while i screamed myself hoarse /

iv

... here in idle moments throughout the night i held long conversations with a visiting desert jerboa / who made a living in an adjacent washbasin cabinet / venturing out only if i sat very very still /

... more than once i questioned him / *shouldn't you be hibernating or aestivating / whichever /*

... *what* / the jerboa would retort each time / *& miss this bounty / no way /*

... *you & i / we have both endured much / we have been singed within an inch of our lives / until there are no new lives we will inhabit / horizons we will never straddle / while the world tiptoes past /*

... i see in you a soul mate / you & me / we have both been crisped & toasted & spat out /
... awaiting dawn to end our nightmares / alongside you my companion i await the birth of
light /
... i await dawn's pigeon flocks /

v

... & as promised dawn delivers the hungry pigeons / intent on distant granaries
/ to whom the whirring meat grinder blades across their flight path are a blur / &
they fly smack into the arrays of air intake fans / splat / thus squandering the many
splendoured plumages of their lives / leaving for me to scrape off the floor / & for
the desert creature to feast / i see him now hopping from one paw to the other in
anticipation & joy /

vi

... & yet each morning arrives unadorned & free / as it surely must come for all
captives of the night / to liberate them to just one more day / to survive not because
of themselves / but / that their suffering is yet incomplete /
... o protect me from my mind / only one prayer / o protect me from my mind /
... while an abrasive wind scours the fur off your body / & the suck of soft sand pulls
you under / & still many seasons must pass before the salvation of rain will deliver
you back up / before your green can erupt from where you lay down / last /

vii

... & all that while / a nobody who contained all the sorrows of the world / held up
the sky in place /
... & no one needs the prison experience to know that the worst that can happen to
you while doing time / is being set free

a loved one's crying over long-distance lines

i

>...is the wind   keening
across taut rusting wires
between poles   collapsing
>   at opposite ends

>...is the approach of chain lightning
before the thunderstorm
>   discovers you   bereft

>...is the suck of riptide   viewed from below
the undertow you topple into
>   headfirst

ii
(overheard conversation at a public phone booth)

she tells him

>   *...all that was in the past*
>   *i am betrothed now*
>   *forget us...*

we lean closer
>   catch the sob

in times of war   we bake plaster lemons

on the 3rd war month
i stumbled upon a wilting lemon
at the back of the fridge
& naturally
since there were no more to be had
made a plaster cast of it

the half dozen clones were then spray painted
a hint of lime green
infused with fresh fruit juice

suddenly it seemed that the truncated supply orchards
were once again in full bloom

or so it seemed
& the illusion sustained us
for weeks
fooling our visitors & neighbours alike
before we reluctantly gave one to each

only to discover
we had run out of lemons
& the orchards run dry

gardens bloomed wherever abaji lived

Anas bin Malik narrated that the prophet Muhammad said, "there is not a pomegranate which does not have a pip from one of the pomegranates of the garden (of Jannah) in it" (Abu Nu'aim).

the fact that i should outlive my father by fifty years
        astounds me no end
as much as it saddens me
        that none of his gardens are still in bloom

i who once caught him weeping to a thumri
        where in his rough short life of a mechanic
        did he acquire the esthetic?
i who once witnessed him empty the entire contents of his pockets
        into a beggar's hands

i who once watched him peel a snake off an orange
        the orange firmly held in the left
        the knife deliberating from the right
liberating the peel's snug wrap from rind
        the snake falls unraveled onto the plate
        still winding & unwinding
            writhing hypnotic of its own volition

oranges would be just one
        in a long line of fruits he once grew
as gardens blossomed wherever we lived
        even when our residence was the desert itself
& when it came time to retire
        & plant his orchard out of the soil that birthed him
he began with the oranges
        he loved the blood red ones best
        preferring them tart
        believing they would nourish our blood

the lemons went in next
& where the soil was well-drained
       he planted pomegranates
       framed by guavas

however   the fruit closest to his heart was the mango
       they were to showcase his orchard
& when feasting on a particularly delicious variety
       we would see him rush out of the house
& bury the dripping half eaten mango
       deep
in his lifetime he planted several rows of them
       quoting
       a grandfather plants a mango tree
       for his grandchildren to feast

       now
as i enter the final phase of my life
       his hand rests on my shoulder
       even as the mango trees are all felled
& his love sees me head out
       open-armed & open-hearted
       in the grace that he was

grandchildless

i who once watched the snake   uncoil deliberately
i who was not allowed to hold the knife
       just yet

I am the painter of eye reflections

The tyrant's army of propaganda artists tirelessly crisscross his vast domains, painting and refreshing inspirational murals celebrating the biographical details of his heroic public life. One such painter in his employ has other ideas.

in the battle of sand & heat
      my weapon of choice is blistering paint

& our legion of groomers   when left alone
      trade boasts
      the one who does the whorls of the ears
          has his leader's attention
      he who models those succulent film star lips
          has the say of matters unsaid
& I
      am a painter of eye reflections
      I am the one   uniquely positioned
      to filter   his grandiose visions

look closely here
      where limpid iris   meets unabashed lash
      there is now a whole new set of crosshatches
          scaffoldings
          swirling webs of nooses
          tossed crosses
& that spray of diffused highlights   right here
      in each   lies a minute iris   staring back
      each   a proclamation in plain sight
          baring the inevitable truth
          of cataclysms still to come

here is the conquering hero on horseback
      racing into battle
      wielding swords & kalashnikovs
      shoulders rocket launchers

here he is   racing a jet into the skirmish
        all the while leering at the camera
        his teeth bared   a painful shade of bright

did you notice the downward facing   hail of bullets

his every deception   carries its echo
        the hero can't get it up
        his wives have fled
        abuses children
        cross dresses
        is up to his eyeballs in amphetamines
        bids mann o salva at will
        triple checks each locked door
        loads & reloads the pistol under his pillow
        sleeps with his eyes open

& to think   for this I spent
        three whole years & five months at art school
honing my skill set
        diligently studying art histories
        phases & revivals
        theories of colour
        monotone to 3-D modelling
        realism to abstract to cartoon
        murals to canvas to graffiti
        pencil oil acrylic spray water
        three years & five months is a lifetime
& to end up a mere itinerant signboard toucher-upper
        who dares to call himself an *artist*

I am here to tell you
        I am *not* a mere functionary
but   I can differentiate
        between the smell of sweet oranges & apples
            & the stench of sarin gas
        it is in moments like these
I have to remind myself   I am better off here
        than my first cousin
        plucked from final year of music school
        to play trombone for life
        following the despot
        in endless official ceremonies
        even when unable to fully close his tunic
or my friend the lighting man
        ex-appropriated from trade school
        to keep the murals glowing
        day & night
        while roadside hovels in the vicinity
            still lie in dark

in our aggregated dedication to our art
        we all are craftsmen great & small
our brush trombone & floodlight
        enrolled into a grand orchestra
that holds up a screen for him
        to project his mad visions
while we play cacophonies of the death march

even though his multitude minions
        sew their gossip   under their eyelids
        lest   they spill it all in sleep
his desperation feasts
        for breakfast on his enemies progeny
while he feeds his mastiffs fresh albacore
hoards jaziya gathered from orphans

& wanders palace hallways labyrinthine
        dressed in drag
converses with former nemesis
        long since quartered & burned as heretics
            their ashes dispersed in the winds
& tirelessly pumps a dozen rounds into his death mask
        snickering from the shadows

already
he hears the edifice groan
        under its bloat
while mongrels howl in the wilderness of his nights
        his whimsical & broadcast baritone
            whimpering into whine

where   I
        once a proud painter of eye reflections
            can sense
        my airbrushing days coming to an end

& speaking of publishing / the monopoly of ink

the monopoly of ink (01)

the kleptomaniacs had always coveted
    the lilt resonance pitch
    of my speech
and left me unable to speak
    of their denouement
they cut out my mother tongue
    and left me theirs
it does not fit my mouth
    it pours lead into every ear
    it robs my dreams of colour
        instead of green sap rising
        there is now this grey metallic tang
            and the resounding of steel

here all my rainsongs shrivel

how do i now
    speak to my mother
    or sing homespun lullabies
        to my unborn

how will i daily shape these stones
    to earn my keep

the monopoly of ink (02)

& now that my tongue has regrown
i speak hybridity
   numerous of minds
here
   here
      &
        HERE
& must now learn to break through
   this chokehold
   over ink
   over eyes
   over ears
   over mouths
where my cry begins as a whimper
   & becomes a scream that no one wants to hear
where oceans of ink are spilled
   to tell *only* one story over & over
      everywhere

The Monopoly of Ink (03)

        Sorry, so sorry

Proclaims the Merchant of Inks

        Sorry, we have just used up our last few drops of ink
        To publish five outstanding & critically reviewed original works
        The first is a slim travelogue titled 'My Week with the Dalai Lama'
        We followed that with a million accounts
        Of Small-Town girls who come to the Big City, make it big & find love & 'fulfillment'
        Seebeesee called the series '…highly original, at times even heartfelt'
        This was followed by our five volumes on the lives of Memsahibs of Lucknow
        Our pen-ultimate publication was Jan Yomesh's extended reflections on eating the apple's core
        &, our final was a masterwork
        Elaine Walk-Tall's Encounters With the Remaining Moth Species of Southeastern
        Falklands
        Did you read that one?

I honestly have no idea how I missed these intriguing titles.
Did all those women really find 'love & fulfillment?'

        All excellent, extensively reviewed works
        By the way, what are you promoting?

Me?
Oh, mine is a dramatization of the voyages of an unmoored & cursed ship plying
amniotic seas
denied every beckoning port of call

        Oh that
        The Greeks got to that harbour first, didn't they?

Yeah, so true
How about an account of a lush Eden from which we were banished
To eternally wander the earth & the seas

        Been there, done that
        Not the right fit
        Sorry
        So sorry

Hey, wait a minute
Would you be interested in seven interlinked short stories
Set over a single cycle of seasons in the charming town of Kotli in the backwaters of
Punjab

Hanh?

It has magical realism violence music & recipes for esoteric & exotic foods

Uhn-huhn

A dog barks, twice
Two of the twenty-odd characters might get laid

Hmm, let me see if I got this right
You said backwater Poonjab?
Where exactly is this, er... Kotli?

parting words

I humbly acknowledge that this work was written by an immigrant settler on the traditional, ancestral, and unceded lands of the following nations that have welcomed us here: Musqueam, Squamish, Tsleil-Waututh, Kwikwetlem, Katzie, Kwantlen, Matsqui, and Sumas of the Stó:lō nations.

Since my natural poetic state is concrete ekphrastics, I have included several inspirational images here (mostly from my family archives) to convey the essence of this book. Each image continues to inform my writing.

My continued gratitude to the care and attention to detail lavished upon my books from the extraordinary team at Caitlin Press. And a very warm thanks also to Dr. Prabhjot Parmar (UFV) for early encouragement and guidance throughout in compiling these poems, and for framing this work in her foreword.

Different versions of some of some of these writing have appeared earlier in the pages of Medium and under *The Polyglot* magazine.

In translating the late Punjabi/French poet Laeeq Babri's Punjabi collection of spare blank verse, *Ghughu Korhe* (Mute Horses), I owe a deep debt to my former mentor and his early redirection towards lean blank verse. On giving me a personal copy of his work, he quoted Jean-Paul Sartre's *écrire, c'est donner* (to write, is to give).

This work is my best effort to incorporate this instruction into my life's guiding principles.

about the author

For the past four decades, Vancouver-based author Tāriq Malik has worked across poetry, fiction, and visual arts, to distil immersive and compelling narratives that are always original and intriguing. He writes intensely in response to the world in flux around him and of his place in its shadows. Born in Pakistani Punjab, he came reluctantly late to these shores. To get here, he first had to survive three wars, two migrations, and two decades in the Kuwaiti desert. He loves landscapes, bodies of living water large and small, and readers and listeners, and claims he writes so that he has something to read on Open Mike at the local Poet's Corner or on the hallowed grounds of public libraries. Tāriq is the author of *Rainsongs of Kotli,* 2004 and *Chanting Denied Shores,* 2010. His first book of poetry, *Exit Wounds,* was published by Caitlin Press in 2022.

All comments are welcomed at:

derektmalik@gmail.com / Twitter (X): @ *TāriqMalik0_0* / Medium: *https://medium. com/@ Tāriqjmalik* / This Lit Life (YouTube): *https://www.youtube.com/channel/ UCx7eSDC8ayojlwqs1nm77gw/*